20th Century
PERSPECTIVES

The Korean War

Michael Burgan

Heinemann Library
Chicago, Illinois

Customer Service 888-454-2279
Visit our website at www.heinemannlibrary.com

Design by Heinemann Library
Maps by John Fleck
Production by Que Net
Printed in China by WKT Company Limited.

07 06 05 04 03
10 9 8 7 6 5 4 3 2 1

Library of Congress Cataloging-in-Publication Data
Burgan, Michael.
  The Korean war / Michael Burgan.
    v. cm. -- (20th-century perspectives)
Includes index.
Contents: The two Koreas -- The background -- The two Koreas emerge --
Moving closer to war -- Attack on the South -- Wartime leaders -- The
Pusan perimeter -- From Inchon to the Yalu river -- The Chinese
counterattack -- The American home front -- Coming to a halt -- Weapons
of the war -- Prisoners of war -- Diplomacy in Korea, politics at home
-- The Korean people and the war -- Later battles -- Peace at last --
The results of the war -- The two Koreas after the war.
  ISBN 1-4034-1144-1 (hardcover) -- ISBN 1-4034-3857-9 (paperback)
  1. Korean War, 1950-1953--Juvenile literature. 2. Korea
(South)--Juvenile literature. 3. Korea (North)--Juvenile literature.
4. Korea--History--Juvenile literature. [1. Korean War, 1950-1953.] I.
Title. II. Series.
  DS918 .B86 2003
  951.904'2--dc21
                                    2002152946

Acknowledgments
The publisher is grateful to the following for permission to reproduce copyright material:
p. 5 Yun Jai-Hyoung/AP Wide World Photo; pp. 6, 20, 23, 36, 37 Hulton Archive/Getty Images; pp. 7, 12, 22, 26, 29, 31, 38, 40 Bettmann/Corbis; p. 8L John Florea/TimePix; p. 8R Department of Defense/TimePix; p. 9 Carl Mydans/TimePix; pp. 10, 27, 33, 35 National Archives and Records Administration; p. 11 Eastfoto/Sovfoto; p. 13 Hulton-Deutsch Collection/Corbis; p. 14 Harry S. Truman Library and Museum; p. 15 Carl Mydans/TimePix; pp. 16, 18, 30, 43 Department of Defense; p. 24 Corbis; p. 25 U. S. Army Military History Institute; p. 28 John Springer Collection/Corbis; p. 32 Margaret Bourke-White/TimePix; p. 39 John Dominis/TimePix; p. 41 HO/World Vision Japan/AP Wide World Photo; p. 42 AFP/Corbis

Cover photograph by Corbis

Special thanks to Colonel Guy A. LoFaro, United States Army, FORSCOM, for his comments in the preparation of this book.

Every effort has been made to contact copyright holders of any material reproduced in this book. Any omissions will be rectified in subsequent printings if notice is given to the publishers.

Some words are shown in bold, **like this.** You can find out what they mean by looking in the glossary.

Contents

The Two Koreas

CHINA

Chongjin

NORTH KOREA

Yalu R.

Taedong R.

Pyongyang★

Imjin R.

•Wonsan

38°

Inchon•

★Seoul

Han R.

SOUTH KOREA

Naktong R.

•Pusan

JAPAN

0 100 200 miles

0 150 300 kilometers

This map shows North Korean and South Korea and the location of the Demilitarized Zone.

Along the border between North Korea and South Korea runs a strip of land about 2.5 mi. (4 km) wide and 151 mi. (248 km) long. This area, created in 1953, is called the **Demilitarized Zone** (DMZ). Neither country can station soldiers or weapons in the zone. But just beyond the barbed wire that marks the DMZ's boundaries, North Korean and South Korean soldiers, along with U.S. Army soldiers on the southern border, watch each other through binoculars while toting machine guns. Former U.S. president Bill Clinton once called the zone the scariest place on Earth.

The two Koreas, joined by armies from around the world, once fought each other near the zone. In June 1950, troops from **communist** North Korea launched a surprise attack on South Korea. The United Nations (UN), with major support from the United States, rushed to South Korea's aid. When the war ended three years later, the two Koreas remained separate, with the DMZ in place. The suspicions and tensions from that period have not gone away. Today, more than 1.7 million North Korean and South Korean troops are stationed within a short drive of the DMZ.

The Cold War

The Korean War grew out of the results of World War II (1939–1945) in Asia. Both the Soviet Union and the United States had troops in Korea in late 1945. Each **superpower** wanted a future Korean government that followed its political and economic system. By 1948, Korea was officially split in two. The north was tied to the Soviet Union, which had a communist government, and the south to the United States. North Korea, however, wanted to unite the Korean **peninsula** under its communist rule. Soviet leader Joseph Stalin supported this goal. So did Mao Zedong, the leader of communist China and a Soviet **ally.**

In the United States, fear of communism and the Soviet Union ran deep after World War II because the Soviets had stated that their goal was to destroy capitalism and dominate the world. Starting in the late 1940s, U.S. foreign policies focused on stopping the spread of communism and weakening the Soviet Union. These policies shaped the **Cold War** between the United States and the Soviet Union, in which each raced to build the most powerful weapons and spread influence around the globe.

A real war in Korea

For the United States and the Soviet Union, the Cold War was mostly **ideological**—a battle of words and ideas. Instead of engaging in combat, the Soviets backed almost any military effort that attacked U.S. interests around the world. In turn, the U.S. supported other countries' armies that battled those Soviet-backed communist forces. Korea was an example of this.

Along the DMZ, South Korean troops, alongside U.S. troops, keep constant watch on the activity of North Korean soldiers.

In Korea, the ideological battle led to a bloody war. Several million North Koreans and South Koreans died during the war. Chinese and American troops faced each other across frozen fields, and soldiers from more than a dozen other countries also served. Over 100,000 troops also faced hunger and disease—or worse—while prisoners of war. Today, U.S. troops are still stationed in South Korea because some world leaders are fearful of North Korea's military power. The Korean War and the world it shaped are important parts of America's past—and its future.

THE TWO KOREAS

	South	North
Official Name	Republic of Korea	Democratic People's Republic of Korea
Capital	Seoul	Pyongyang
Area	37,900 sq. mi. (98,157 sq. km)	46,400 sq. mi. (120,171 sq. km)
Population (as of 2001)	47.9 million	27.9 million
Government	Democratic republic	Communist republic

The Background

The two Koreas share a recorded history that goes back more than 2,000 years. In around 100 B.C.E., Chinese forces invaded the northern end of the peninsula. Over time, the Chinese brought their culture, religions, and government system, dominating life there for centuries.

Japan takes over

During the 1590s, leaders in Japan saw that Korea had great geographic value for its plans to expand onto mainland Asia. Japanese forces invaded the peninsula, hoping to use it as a base for attacks on China. Korea became a battleground for Chinese and Japanese forces. In the late 1890s, Japan sent troops to Korea to extend Japanese influence over the southern part of the peninsula. By this time, China was no longer a major power in Asia, but other countries were trying to gain control. Russia shared an 11-mi. (17.7-km) border with northern Korea, and it wanted to gain power in that region.

After 1910, Japanese police officers such as these helped enforce Japan's rule over Korea.

From 1904 to 1905, Japan and Russia fought a war over their competing interests in Korea and Manchuria, a region of China that bordered both Korea and Russia. After a important victory, Japan arose as the major military power in East Asia. After taking control of Korea in 1907, Japan officially **annexed** the country in 1910, turning it into a colony called Choson. Many Japanese settled there, and the government forced the people to learn Japanese and adopt their customs.

Many people despised Japanese rule, and some called for independence. In 1919, a protest against the Japanese turned violent. At least 6,000 protesters were killed and many more were taken prisoner. Japan, however, continued its harsh practices, and in 1931, it used Korea as a base for an attack on Manchuria. By 1937, large parts of China were under Japanese control.

U.S. troops arrive in Seoul, Korea, on September 8, 1945, as part of the American occupation.

Korea and World War II

Japan's actions in East Asia eventually led to a Japanese attack on Pearl Harbor, Hawaii. The December 7, 1941, bombing brought the United States into World War II. The Americans and the Soviets were part of the Allied forces, with a common enemy in Europe: **Nazi** Germany, ruled by Adolf Hitler. The United States and the Soviet Union put aside their differences to defeat Hitler.

In Asia and the islands of the Pacific Ocean, the United States led the fight against the Japanese. In 1945, Soviet troops marched into Manchuria, defeated the Japanese forces there, and then moved to Korea.

The United States. saw that the Soviets could easily take over the peninsula. Not wanting **communists** to have control of Korea, the Americans proposed splitting Korea in half along the **38th parallel.** The Soviets agreed, and their forces stopped there. A few weeks later, after the end of World War II, U.S. troops entered the southern part of the peninsula. The stage was set for two separate Koreas.

The Hermit Kingdom meets the West

Starting in the 1600s, Korea was largely under the control of the Manchu dynasty of China. Korea was sometimes called the Hermit Kingdom because the Manchus kept it isolated from foreign countries. In 1871, a U.S. ship sailed into Pyongyang, hoping to trade with the Koreans. The Koreans attacked the ship, killing the crew. A few years later, the United States responded. As a group of U.S. Marines landed in Seoul and took over several forts. Relations between the two nations improved in 1882, when they signed a trade agreement.

The Two Koreas Emerge

At first, the two Koreas were ruled by military governors. In the south, U.S. General John Reed Hodge was in charge. Under Hodge, the U.S. government did not accept the "people's committee" that had sprung up to run local affairs. The committee members included both **communists** and noncommunists who had opposed Japanese rule. The Americans preferred to work with Koreans who were actively anticommunist and had ties to the United States. One of these people, Syngman Rhee, returned from **exile** to run the government in the south. In northern Korea, the Soviets also put an exile in power. Kim Il Sung was a communist who had fought the Japanese during the 1930s.

Syngman Rhee, (left) the first president of South Korea, and Kim Il Sung, the communist ruler of North Korea.

The two leaders

Both Syngman Rhee and Kim Il Sung had opposed Japanese rule of Korea. Their lives, however, took very different paths. Rhee, born in 1875, studied in the United States and lived there for many years. Rhee was strongly anticommunist and usually supported American interests, but his harsh rule sometimes made U.S. officials uncomfortable. Rhee served as president of the Republic of Korea until 1960. He died in 1965 while living in Hawaii.

Kim was born in 1912 and lived for a time in Manchuria. He was there when Japan seized control in 1931, and Kim organized a **guerrilla** force to fight the Japanese. Kim also lived in the Soviet Union, where he became a dedicated communist. During World War II, he fought for the Soviets and won the rank of major. Kim ruled North Korea as a tightly controlled communist state until his death in 1994.

Ruling the two Koreas

In the south, Rhee led a political organization called the Korean Democratic Party. Some of the party members had supported the Japanese when they ruled Korea. Many Koreans in the south opposed Rhee because of these ties to their hated former rulers. Others disliked Rhee's support of the wealthy classes. Rhee tried to suppress any political activity that challenged his government. Police arrested or beat people who opposed Rhee and his policies. Violence erupted several times in the south, as opponents fought against Rhee's forces and his supporters. Some of the violence was also tied to the American presence in the country, as many South Koreans wanted independence.

In the north, Kim worked closely with the Soviet Union to set up a communist government. The Soviets broadcast **propaganda,** telling the people "The Soviet government is the highest form of democracy." As Kim took control, he jailed or killed some of his political opponents; others fled to the south. In both parts of Korea, the ruling parties tried to shape postwar Korea along strict **ideological** lines, and they denied average citizens a role in running the government.

Elections and violence

At first, the Soviet Union and the United States had pledged to allow elections across the Korean peninsula to choose a new national government. By 1947, however, the two countries could not agree on how to run these elections. The United States finally handed the problem to the United Nations (UN). The Soviet

South Korean troops take cover as they try to end a revolt against Syngman Rhee's rule.

Union refused to let the UN conduct elections in the north, so only southern voters went to the polls in May 1948. Rhee was chosen president of the new Republic of Korea (ROK), which officially formed on August 15. A few weeks later, the North Koreans set up their own country, the Democratic People's Republic of Korea (DPRK), with Kim as its leader. Although the country was called democratic, Kim and the **Communist Party** controlled North Korea.

Both Rhee and Kim sought a united Korea—with each man hoping to be in charge. Kim stirred up trouble in the south, supporting local communists. But some South Koreans opposed Rhee and his government on their own, without any support from Kim. Even before the May 1948 elections, an uprising had started on the southern island of Cheju. Later in the year, a rebellion broke out in the city of Yosu. **Guerrillas** operated in the south through 1949. A New York Times reporter wrote that large areas were "darkened . . . by a cloud of terror that is probably unparalleled in the world."

Fighting broke out along the **38th parallel.** Sometimes North Korea encouraged South Koreans to rebel or its troops attacked ROK forces. Other times, South Korea started the violence, attacking North Korean troops. In one sense, the trouble on the peninsula was becoming a civil war, as Koreans struggled to reunite themselves. Most U.S. and Soviet troops had left the peninsula by June 1949, but each of the two Koreas was dependent on ideological and military support from the superpowers. To some Americans, the growing conflict in Korea was about U.S. interests versus Soviet interests in Asia.

Moving Closer to War

After World War II, the Soviet Union and communism became a growing menace to the United States. By 1948, the Soviet Union controlled large parts of Eastern Europe, and it supported the **communist** forces that won a civil war in China the next year. The Soviet Union also joined the United States as a **nuclear** power by testing its first nuclear weapon in August 1949. U.S. scientists soon began working on a more powerful nuclear weapon, a **hydrogen bomb,** in an effort to stay ahead of the Soviet Union.

Americans also felt threatened at home by concerns that the United States itself was filled with communists. Those fears arose after World War II, with reports that some past U.S. officials were communists. Another shock came early in 1950, when the country learned that scientists from both Great Britain and the United States had given the Soviets information on how to build an atomic bomb. Around the world, U.S. officials saw every conflict as part of the growing Cold War. The developing events in Korea seemed part of that pattern.

The blast of a nuclear weapon creates a distinct mushroom-shaped cloud. The successful Soviet test of a nuclear bomb in 1949 raised fears in the United States.

Preparing for war

The Soviet Union was glad to see communism take control in China. The Soviet leader, Joseph Stalin, also wanted to keep a friendly government ruling North Korea. Stalin, however, was not the driving force behind the Korean War. Instead, Kim Il Sung pushed for an invasion of the south. Several times during 1949, Kim asked for Soviet support in a war on South Korea. Stalin said no.

Kim refused to give up. In April 1950, he made a secret visit to the Soviet capital, Moscow. This time, when he asked permission to launch a war, Stalin said yes. The Chinese leader, Mao, also backed the war. Stalin felt more able to confront the Americans, since he had a new ally in Asia—China—and nuclear weapons. U.S. government statements may have also given Stalin and Mao some of their confidence. In January 1950, U.S. Secretary of State Dean Acheson said that the United States would respond to military attacks in certain parts of Asia, but he did not include South Korea on the list.

Chinese leader Mao Zedong (right) and the Soviet Union's Joseph Stalin (left) meet in Moscow several months before they approve Kim Il Sung's plan for a war in Korea.

The final steps

With Stalin's approval, Kim prepared for war. He had a well-trained army. Many North Korean communists had fought for the Soviet Union during World War II. Up to 100,000 North Koreans had also helped Mao's forces win the civil war in China. The DPRK forces had a wide assortment of Soviet weapons, including T–34 tanks and heavy **artillery.** Stalin did not want to make it obvious that the Soviet Union was involved in the attack, so he pulled back Soviet advisers from the **38th parallel** before the war began. From a distance, the Soviet advisors continued to play a major role in planning the war, agreeing on a date for the invasion of South Korea: June 25, 1950.

Dean Acheson's Speech

In Korea, we have taken great steps which have ended our military occupation, and in cooperation with the United Nations, we have established an independent and sovereign country recognized by nearly all the rest of the world. . .There is a new day which has dawned in Asia. It is a day in which the Asian peoples are on their own, and know it, and intend to continue on their own. . .We are their friends . . . but we can only help where we are wanted and only where the conditions of help are really sensible and possible.

From Dean Acheson's 1950 speech on the "defensive perimeter," defining U.S. interests in Asia.

Attack on the South

Around 4:00 A.M. on June 25, 1950, North Korean **artillery** guns boomed along the western edge of the boundary separating the two Koreas. Thousands of troops from the North Korean People's Army (NKPA) and about 150 Soviet-made tanks then rolled into South Korea. It was Sunday, and many ROK soldiers were home for the weekend. The ones stationed at the **38th parallel** were outnumbered and outgunned by the North Koreans who swarmed over the border.

United States Marines pass by a burning building during the early days of the war.

The North Koreans met some resistance at several spots, but for the most part, they tore through the ROK forces. ROK artillery shells bounced off the NKPA's tanks, and the ROK had no tanks of its own. Hong An, a student in Seoul at the time, later remembered hearing "a remote roaring noise from the north" when the invasion began. South Korean troops scrambled to defend Seoul, while the government called to the world for support.

The war begins: the American response

Hours after the invasion began, the South Korean ambassador asked the United States for help. President Harry Truman and his advisors decided to ask for a special meeting of the **Security Council,** the most powerful arm of the United Nations (UN). The next day, the council voted to condemn the North Korean attack, and two days later the Security Council agreed to send an international force to aid the South Koreans.

America returns to battle

In public statements, North Korea insisted its invasion was in response to new South Korean attacks on its forces. The Soviet Union backed this version of the events and assured Truman it had not helped the North Koreans. Truman and his advisers, however, did not believe either claim.

The UN Security Council voted to send troops to help defend South Korea against the invading North Koreans. The UN representative from the Soviet Union was not present.

In a public address to the U.S. Truman told Americans why the new war was so important to national interests: "The fact that communist forces have invaded Korea is a warning that there may be similar acts of aggression in other parts of the world."

U.S. officials believed the Korean invasion was meant to direct American attention away from Europe. They expected some sort of Soviet military move there. In the meantime, acting before the UN-approved military action, the U.S. military rushed to send troops and weapons to South Korea. U.S. Navy ships picked up Americans fleeing the war, while planes flew overhead, scouting for the enemy and offering protection. On June 27, American jets shot down several North Korean planes. Barely five years after the end of World War II, the U.S. was at war again.

The United Nations

The United Nations was formed on October 24, 1945, right after World War II. Its primary goals are to prevent global conflicts and to protect human rights. The UN has several agencies and councils. The largest, the General Assembly, has representatives from all the member nations. The fifteen-member Security Council includes the permanent members and ten countries that sit on the council for two years at a time.

The Korean War marked the first time that the UN organized a military force to try to end an international conflict. Today, the UN has peacekeeping troops in several countries around the world.

Wartime Leaders

As the Korean War began, the United States relied on the skills of a number of political and military leaders. Three men, however, had key roles in directing the American response to the war in Korea.

President Harry Truman

Once the owner of a Kansas City, Missouri, clothing store, Harry Truman (1884–1972) had a long career in politics before President Franklin D. Roosevelt chose him as his running mate for the 1944 presidential election. With Roosevelt's death in April 1945, Truman had the task of leading the United States through the end of World War II. In August, he made the historic decision to drop two atomic bombs on Japan.

Harry Truman faced a close presidential election in 1948, then dealt with the challenges of confronting the Soviet Union and China during the Korean War.

After the war, Truman oversaw the U.S. policy of **containment.** As the Cold War began, Truman and his advisers wanted to contain **communism** where it already existed instead of letting it spread. One way to do this, Truman believed, was to send money and supplies to any country threatened by a communist takeover. This policy was called the Truman Doctrine.

When the Korean War began, Truman did not ask Congress to declare war. Instead he used his power as commander in chief of the military to send U.S. forces into battle. Truman called the fighting a "police action" Congress supported the move and did not question his decision. Over time, however, Truman faced more complaints about his handling of the war.

President Truman speaks

If we let Korea down, the Soviet [Union] will keep right on going and swallow up one piece of Asia after another . . . and no telling what would happen in Europe.

General Douglas MacArthur

Early in July 1950, the United Nations gave Truman the power to name the commander of UN forces in Korea. The president named General Douglas MacArthur (1880–1964), a hero during World War II who helped create the strategy that defeated the Japanese. He was serving as the military governor of Japan and commander of U.S. forces in the Far East when the Korean War began. U.S. troops in Japan were not prepared for battle; they acted more like a police force than an army and did not train heavily. Still, these were the first troops MacArthur could send to South Korea at the start of the war.

Syngman Rhee also placed his troops under MacArthur's command. Even before this, MacArthur had visited South Korea and saw that the ROK army was not equipped to fight off the invaders. He also realized U.S. naval and air power would not be enough to help America's ally. Only large ground forces—soldiers, tanks, and guns—could defeat the North Koreans. Truman agreed with MacArthur's strategy—at least at first. As the war went on, the president and the general sometimes had different goals.

"In war," Douglas MacArthur once said, "there is no substitute for victory." In his battle plans for Korea, the general did not rule out anything—including the use of nuclear weapons.

Secretary of State Dean Acheson

As secretary of state, Dean Acheson (1893–1971) was President Truman's key advisor on foreign affairs. In that role, Acheson took much of the blame for the country's troubles overseas. After communist forces won China's civil war, some Americans accused Acheson and the State Department of "losing" China, since the former Chinese government had been a close U.S. **ally.**

The secretary also played an important role in shaping America's first Cold War policies. These included the Truman Doctrine and the Marshall Plan. The Marshall Plan, launched in 1948, gave billions of dollars in U.S. aid to European countries. This money was supposed to help the Europeans rebuild their economies after World War II and resist communism.

The Pusan Perimeter

Ground forces from the United States saw their first action in Korea early in July 1950. By this time, the NKPA had captured Seoul and was pushing farther south. Like the ROK troops, the first U.S. soldiers lacked weapons that could destroy North Korea's tanks. The Americans slowed the invaders somewhat, but they could not stop them. In early reports, U.S. officials admitted the North Koreans were "first-class" soldiers.

Throughout July, the UN sent more troops and equipment to Korea. These included navy ships from Great Britain and Canada, and Australian pilots flying U.S. planes based in Japan. The U.S. military force had shrunk considerably from its 12 million troops at the end of World War II. Now, only 600,000 troops were in uniform, including those stationed in Europe. Truman sent thousands of troops to South Korea but also gave MacArthur permission to use all military forces available in the U.S. and the Pacific. Truman then ordered a military **draft** to build up more forces for the future.

The 24th Infantry Regiment, an African-American unit, heads for battle. By June 1953, about 51,000 African Americans—including some women—were stationed in Korea and Japan.

Trying to win time

In the first few weeks of the war, South Korea provided most of the ground troops and suffered heavy losses. By one account, the ROK lost 44,000 men—either killed, captured, or missing in action—in just the first week. More Americans arrived in the first weeks of July, along with U.S. aircraft. These planes scored a major victory on July 10, 1950, knocking out dozens of North Korean tanks and trucks. U.S. air power was an important factor in slowing the NKPA advance and buying time so that more UN and U.S. soldiers and weapons could reach the **peninsula.**

The battlefield became chaotic at times, as **refugees** fled from the advancing North Koreans. These people, along with wrecked vehicles, filled the roads, slowing the advance of UN forces. The Americans and their allies also faced **guerrillas.** Some were North Koreans who had crossed the **38th parallel,** but others were South Koreans who opposed President Rhee and welcomed the NKPA invasion.

In mid-July, the United States suffered heavy **casualties** around the city of Taejon. Adding to the defeat was the loss of General William F. Dean. Separated from his men, he was taken prisoner and held until the end of the war. Despite the losses, the fighting at Taejon gave the United States even more time to bring in troops. By the beginning of August, about 47,000 soldiers were in and around South Korea.

This map shows the path of the North Korean invasion and the position of UN forces at the Pusan Perimeter.

Pulling back to Pusan

The UN forces eventually fell back into the southeastern corner of the Korean peninsula. Their defenses set up a line called the Pusan **Perimeter.** Pusan was the major seaport of the region, where U.S. troops and supplies arrived. From the city, the forces rushed up to defend the perimeter, which extended from about 40 to 100 mi. (64 to 161 km) beyond Pusan. By August, the total UN forces outnumbered the North Koreans, and they had more large tanks and artillery. The UN forces also controlled the skies over South Korea and the waters that surrounded it on three sides.

African Americans in Korea

In 1948, President Harry Truman signed an order to fully **integrate** the U.S. armed forces. For the first time, white and African-American soldiers would live, fight, and sometimes die together on the battlefield. By the time the Korean War started, however, the troops were still **segregated.**

One of the first American units to reach South Korea was the all-black 24th Infantry Regiment of the 25th Division. These soldiers took part in the first successful UN counterattack of the war. Despite this bravery, black soldiers continued to face racism on the battlefield. Finally, in October 1951, the troops in Korea were integrated. During the war, more than 3,000 African Americans gave their lives for their country, almost 10 percent of total U.S. losses.

From Inchon to the Yalu River

MacArthur's plan was to launch a massive **amphibious** assault behind the North Korean lines. It followed the strategy he had used in World War II—attack the enemy away from its main force, cutting off lines of communication and supplies to the front. Almost from the beginning of the Korean War, MacArthur eyed the city of Inchon as the site for this assault because it "present[ed] an opportunity for a decisive blow."

U.S. Marines climb out their landing craft at Inchon. The Marines had fewer than 200 casualties during the invasion.

The Marines come ashore

The force assembled to attack at Inchon included troops from seven nations; the United States contributed most of the troops and their landing craft. To keep the North Koreans guessing where an amphibious invasion might occur, the Americans bombed and shelled several spots on both the east and west coasts of the **peninsula.** Finally, on September 15, the UN forces struck at Inchon, launching what was called Operation Chromite.

As rain fell, thousand of U.S. Marines led the attack just after dawn. They struck first at Wolmi-do, a small island in the harbor. Other soldiers then landed at Inchon itself. The small NKPA force defending the city was overwhelmed, and MacArthur's troops quickly took control. Several days later, a nearby airfield was also in their hands. Less than a week after the invasion, the UN had 50,000 troops ashore, along with thousands of vehicles and 250,000 tons (226,750 metric tons) of equipment.

To Seoul and beyond

By September 27, the UN forces had recaptured Seoul, though with heavy civilian casualties. By this time, MacArthur's troops had also broken through the North Korean lines at the Pusan **Perimeter** and headed north. The NKPA retreated back across the **38th parallel,** with ROK and UN forces in pursuit. Syngman Rhee now had his chance to reunite the two Koreas with a pro-American, anti**communist** government, a goal MacArthur supported.

The first South Korean troops crossed the 38th parallel in late September. Within several weeks, the North Korean capital of Pyongyang was under UN control. MacArthur's forces continued to race northward, approaching the Yalu River, the border between North Korea and China. What the Americans didn't know was that China was preparing to enter the war, to aid North Korea, and prevent any attack on its soil.

China responds

On October 2, Mao Zedong wrote to Joseph Stalin about Chinese plans to send troops into Korea. They would be called volunteers, but they would actually be under Chinese control. Mao realized the move might lead to a U.S. declaration of war on China. "We must be prepared," Mao wrote, "for the possible bombardments by American air forces of many Chinese cities and industrial bases." Still, Mao was ready to take that risk, and Stalin wanted him to act.

By mid-October, the first Chinese volunteers crossed into North Korea, fighting on the same side as the NKPA. These combined forces carried out scattered attacks, then slipped out of view. U.S. troops continued to move north. As one officer later said, "I really thought we had won the war . . . We went north with high hopes." MacArthur, at the same time, was convinced the Chinese would not enter the war in any meaningful way. He told Truman, "We are no longer fearful of their intervention . . . if the Chinese tried to get down to Pyongyang there would be the greatest slaughter." The American overconfidence turned out to be a costly mistake.

A map showing the Inchon invasion and the extent of the UN control.

Landing at Inchon

The entire beach area simply disappeared in an enormous cloud of dust and smoke with only the occasional glare of a rocket burst showing. It was really awesome . . . The landing craft lined up in waves . . . and when the signal flag dipped, motors were gunned and all surged forward toward the beach.

Lieutenant Frank Muetzel, describing the scene before he landed at Inchon

The Chinese Counterattack

By mid–November, at least 200,000 Chinese troops had crossed the Yalu River, waiting for the UN forces to advance. The Chinese were joined by about 150,000 members of the NKPA and North Korean guerrillas. UN forces in the region numbered about 250,000.

The first attacks

The major Chinese attack started in late November. The weather was already bitterly cold, often dropping below 0 °F (–18 °C). The Chinese struck first at the front of the UN lines, while more Chinese troops waited behind the lines to catch UN troops **retreating.** The Chinese blew bugles and shouted as they charged into battle.

As the Chinese attacked, many American and ROK troops were hit with "bug-out fever." Fearing advancing enemy forces, soldiers ran from the front lines, clinging to any vehicle that could carry them to safety.

On December 6, the Chinese and North Koreans recaptured Pyongyang. The UN soon began preparing to leave Inchon, on the west coast, and Hungnam on the east coast. At Hungnam, 105,000 troops, 98,000 civilians, 17,500 vehicles, and 350,000 tons of cargo were pulled out in just two weeks. By the December 15, the major U.S. force in

American and UN forces head south after the major communist counterattack in North Korea, led by the Chinese.

Korea, the Eighth U.S. Army, set up a defensive line just north of Seoul, knowing the enemy was heading for the South Korean capital. Now, back below the **38th parallel,** the Eighth Army had just made the longest retreat in U.S. military history.

Reaction in the United States

On November 30, President Truman told reporters the United States was "fighting for our national security and our survival." Lucius Battle, an assistant to Secretary of State Acheson, said years later that U.S. officials saw China's entry into the war as a "terrifying situation." At the same time, however, some of Truman's advisers were suggesting the United States should pull out of Korea altogether, saying its value was not worth the risk of huge American losses. On the other side were people like MacArthur, who called for all-out war against the Chinese.

A map showing the Chinese counterattack.

On December 9, Truman wrote that he believed that World War III was about to begin. Although he did not welcome such a war, he was prepared to "meet whatever comes." A week later, he declared a national emergency, calling on Americans to "make a mighty production effort to meet the defense requirements of the nation."

First-hand look at war

*All up and down the river valley, all hell had broken loose. **Tracers** and explosions, left and right. Flares would explode, giving too much light, then flutter down and extinguish themselves in frozen corn stubble. The Chinese blew bugles and whistles and shouted American profanity. I thought their bugles were playing* Silent Night, Holy Night. *Between shots and explosions I could hear the wounded crying for help.*

Jimmy Marks, an American soldier on the front lines during one of the first Chinese attacks.

The American Home Front

When the Korean War began, many Americans believed fighting the **communists** in Korea was the right thing to do. National polls showed 75 percent of Americans approved of sending U.S. troops to Korea. After the Chinese invasion, however, that opinion changed. Only about half the people polled said it was right to have U.S. troops in Korea, and many said it had been a mistake getting involved in the first place. President Truman's popularity fell as Americans realized there would be no quick and easy victory in Korea.

REPUBLICAN
JOSEPH R.
McCARTHY
FOR
U. S.
SENATOR

Before his election to the Senate in 1946, Joseph McCarthy built a reputation for himself as a war hero and was sometimes called Tail Gunner Joe.

Changes at home

After World War II, many returning soldiers married and began raising families. By the time of the Korean War, The United States was in the middle of the Baby Boom, a period of population growth that lasted until the early 1960s. Many of the returning soldiers also went to college, thanks to a federal program that helped pay for their education. As more college graduates found good jobs and started families, they moved to new suburbs being built outside of major cities. In the suburbs, families often enjoyed a new form of entertainment: television. Although TV had been invented before the war, it did not become an important part of American life until the early 1950s.

The Korean War did not pose an immediate threat to this new way of life. But the war did affect how the government spent its money. After World War II, Truman had cut spending on defense. The new conflict forced him to almost triple defense spending between 1950 and 1953, from $17 billion to $50 billion. The boost in government spending created jobs, but it also led to higher wages and prices.

By not asking Congress to declare war, Truman helped strengthen the office of the president. In both World War I and World War II, the presidents had asked Congress to declare war. After Korea, future presidents became more likely to use the military on their own, thanks to their power as commander in chief, instead of getting a formal declaration of war.

The rise of McCarthyism

Throughout the Korean War, the most pressing issue in the United States. was the Cold War and the fear of communism. The arrests of several people accused of spying for the Soviet Union helped fuel these fears. Then, just before the Korean War began, Republican senator Joseph McCarthy of Wisconsin said he had a list of names of known communists working for the U.S. State Department. This charge led to a hunt for communists in government, education, and even the entertainment industry. This movement to find communists—sometimes based on weak or no evidence—was later called **McCarthyism.**

While hundreds of thousands of U.S. troops fought in Korea, most Americans were focused on their work and home lives. The conflict did not receive the same attention from the media as either World War II or the Vietnam War.

During the era of McCarthyism, some innocent people were falsely accused of being communists. Congress also passed a law that required communist groups to register with the government, and no known communist was allowed to travel overseas. The hunt for alleged communists created an atmosphere of suspicion across the country. President Truman attacked McCarthyism, saying "When even one American—who has done nothing wrong—is forced by fear to shut his mind and close his mouth, then all Americans are in peril."

McCarthy's charges did not lead to the conviction of a single person charged with spying, though several Americans had spied for the Soviet Union before and during World War II. The U.S. government did not find out about these people until after the World War II and information about the spying was not made public until the 1990s.

The Rosenberg case

In 1950, Julius and Ethel Rosenberg were two of the Americans charged with spying for the Soviet Union during World War II. Both denied their guilt, but they were convicted in 1951 and executed two years later. The Rosenberg case kept Americans fearful of domestic communism during the Korean War. Some people, however, believed the Rosenbergs were innocent and that they did not receive a fair trial. Later, further evidence confirmed that Julius had been a spy. Ethel had not actively spied, but she did know about her husband's activities.

Coming to a Halt

As 1951 began, the Chinese and North Koreans followed the UN forces back across the **38th parallel,** recapturing Seoul and pushing past the South Korean capital. Finally, in mid-February, the UN stopped the enemy's advance. By this time, China had rejected a UN proposal for a cease fire. The Chinese had introduced several new factors into the war. They wanted a seat in the UN and said U.S. naval ships had to leave the waters off Taiwan. In January 1951, the UN made another offer to discuss peace. It promised to set up a commission—largely friendly to **communist** China—to settle the issue of who represented China at the United Nations. China refused to discuss the UN plan.

The UN strikes back

On December 23, 1950, General Walton Walker, commander of the Eighth U.S. Army, died in a jeep accident. His replacement was Matthew Ridgway, who had fought with distinction during World War II. Ridgway slowly helped the U.S. forces regain their fighting spirit, following the huge losses suffered since the Chinese counterattack.

General Matthew Ridgway (left) was later replaced by General James Van Fleet (right) as commander of the Eighth U.S. Army.

Although Ridgway first had to pull his men farther back into South Korea, his plan was to launch a counterattack of his own, to drive the Chinese back over the 38th parallel. On February 21, 1951, Ridgway began Operation Killer, which was followed by other operations that pushed back the Chinese and NKPA. In March, UN forces retook Seoul and approached the 38th parallel. For a time, Ridgway's troops fought in North Korea as well.

In late April, the Chinese made one last attempt to recapture Seoul. The UN forces lost some ground in the central part of South Korea, but they kept control of the capital. The Chinese suffered 70,000 casualties, compared to about 7,000 for the UN.

U.S. and South Korean troops fire antiaircraft guns at enemy planes. Large field guns, such as mortars and artillery, caused the most casualties during the war.

Battle at the top

As U.S. troops fought along the Korean borders, their leaders engaged in their own battle. Since the Chinese invasion, MacArthur and Truman had argued more about how to fight the war. MacArthur often talked about attacking China directly, or at least ending communist rule in North Korea. Truman was becoming content with merely containing communism at the 38th parallel. He also feared that a wider war with China would lead the Soviet Union to enter the war or begin a new one in Europe.

On April 11, Truman removed MacArthur as the commander of the UN forces and U.S. troops in Asia. Ridgway was appointed as his replacement. Despite losing his position, MacArthur returned home a hero. Removing MacArthur made Truman even more unpopular among U.S. voters.

The end for MacArthur

But you may ask: Why can't we take other steps to punish the aggressor? Why don't we bomb Manchuria and China itself? . . . If we were to do those things, we would be running a very grave risk of starting a general war . . . A number of events have made it evident that General MacArthur did not agree with that policy. I have therefore considered it essential to relieve General MacArthur so that there would be no doubt or confusion as to the real purpose and aim of our policy.

President Harry Truman, April 11, 1951

Weapons of the War

The North Koreans relied on the Soviet Union and the Chinese for their weapons. In most cases, the Soviet Union gave its allies outdated weapons. The Chinese relied on some Soviet guns. They also used weapons they had captured from the Japanese during World War II and U.S. weapons taken from the Nationalists during the Chinese civil war.

The United States also relied on older equipment—some dating back to World War I (1914–1918), but most of it from World War II. During the Korean War, however, the U.S. military introduced new weapons and equipment it had been developing since 1945. These included improved body armor and rockets launched from a soldier's shoulder.

Slightly faster than the MiG 15, F-86 Saberjets such as these, shot down hundreds of enemy planes.

The first jet war

Although both sides flew planes with propellers, the Chinese, Soviets, North Koreans, and UN forces all used jet fighter planes. These planes had first appeared, in small numbers, at the end of World War II. The Korean War marked the first time enemy jet planes engaged in aerial combat.

The Soviet Union would not let the North Koreans or Chinese fly its best jet, the MiG-15. Instead, Soviet pilots flew them, dressed in Chinese uniforms. The planes also had Chinese symbols on their bodies, so the Americans would not know the Soviets were involved in the fighting.

The Soviet planes were only flown near the Yalu River, to reduce the risk of a downed pilot being captured. The Soviet Union never admitted at the time that it used its own pilots. U.S. officials knew they were

Famous fighters

Well-known U.S. jet pilots from the Korean War include Wally Schirra and John Glenn. Both men were later among the first seven U.S. astronauts. Glenn also served as a U.S. senator from Ohio and ran for president. Baseball player Ted Williams also flew jets during the Korean War.

A huge ball of fire marks where a napalm bomb explodes near a North Korean factory. The U.S. military used an average of 50,000 gallons (189,250 liters) of napalm each day of the war.

involved but decided to ignore it, to reduce the risk of an open war with the Soviet Union. U.S. fighter pilots had a major disadvantage, compared to the enemy—they were not allowed to chase **communist** aircraft across the Yalu River. U.S. officials did not want to fight on or above Chinese soil.

Other tactics from the air

Despite the presence of Soviet jets and pilots, U.S. bombers did successfully destroy North Korean cities, factories, and bridges. U.S. pilots also dropped napalm. Also called jellied gas, napalm is a chemical that creates large fires when dropped from planes inside specially designed bombs. The Korean War also saw the first major use of helicopters in battle. The U.S. military used "choppers" to supply troops, move soldiers quickly on the battlefield, rescue trapped forces, and carry the wounded.

Nuclear weapons

At different points during the Korean War, the United States threatened to use **nuclear** weapons, particularly against the Chinese. On November 30, 1950, President Truman said the United States would take any military step necessary to defeat the Chinese. "That includes," he said, "every weapon that we have." General MacArthur asked for the authority to use nuclear weapons, if he thought it was necessary, and he drew up a plan to use several dozen of them. Truman, however, refused to give him that power. Still, in the spring of 1951, Truman approved a request from his top military advisors, the Joint Chiefs of Staff, to allow the use of several **atomic bombs,** in case China sent more troops into Korea.

War of words

During the Korean War, both sides used **propaganda.** Sometimes it was directed at the soldiers in the field. Both sides dropped leaflets urging enemy troops to surrender, or telling them their side was going to lose. This kind of propaganda was also called psychological warfare. Away from the battlefield, the Chinese, Soviets, and North Koreans used propaganda to try to turn other countries against the United States. They claimed the UN used weapons that spread deadly germs, then forced captured POWs to confirm it. The United States denied the claim, and some Soviet documents later showed the charge was part of a propaganda effort.

Prisoners of War

In almost every war, both sides take prisoners, preventing them from rejoining their armies and fighting again. In 1929, most of the world's countries signed the Geneva Convention, which spelled out how prisoners of war (POWs) should be treated. The articles of the Geneva Convention were updated right before the Korean War started, though they did not go into effect until October 1950. POWs were to be treated "humanely." The rules demanded that the sick and wounded receive proper care and that prisoners not be tortured or forced to tell any military secrets.

A scene from the 1962 film The Manchurian Candidate, *a story about the brainwashing of a U.S. POW during the Korean War.*

During the Korean War, China and North Korea said they would follow the rules of the Geneva Convention, though they had not signed it. The United States had signed the treaty, but it had not yet been approved by the U.S. Senate. Both sides chose to ignore parts of the Geneva Convention. The treatment of prisoners and the handling of their release became key issues as the **communist** forces and the UN met to discuss peace.

UN POWs

During the first part of the war, the NKPA was particularly brutal in its treatment of prisoners. Both ROK and UN soldiers who surrendered were sometimes shot. Those who lived might be tortured. POWs were occasionally forced to walk dozens of miles without receiving proper food or medical care. On one of these so-called "death marches," in November 1950, 130 out of 700 UN POWs died. During the first winter of the war, one-third of all American POWs died.

After China entered the war, it took control of most of the UN prisoners. In general, the Chinese were more humane captors than the North Koreans. Still, the tales told by former American POWs suggest starvation and death were a constant fear. Lawrence Bailey was captured at the Chosin Reservoir. He described a ten-day march with the Chinese: "Many of the men were wounded—some of them badly—and all of us were hungry and suffering from frostbite." Soldiers who stopped marching were taken to the woods and shot.

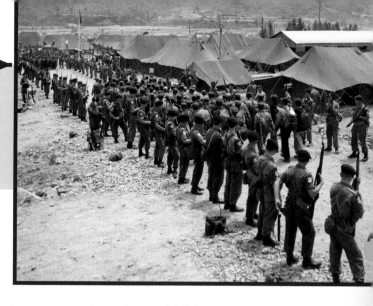

Under the watchful eye of UN guards, communist POWs march through the camp. At the Koje-do camp, weak security and overcrowding led to a POW uprising.

The Chinese hoped to use its somewhat better treatment of POWs in its propaganda. The Chinese also took the opportunity to teach the prisoners about communism and attack American values. Several UN soldiers, including Americans, made broadcasts criticizing UN aims in the war. Twenty-one Americans chose to join the Chinese side.

Some American POWs ended up in the Soviet Union, a fact not openly known until the 1990s. In North Korea, the Soviets used NKPA and Chinese soldiers to question downed pilots. Several dozen of the POWs were then brought to the Soviet Union for more questioning. Many of these Americans were never heard from again.

Chinese and North Korean POWs

The ROK could be just as brutal as the North Koreans with its prisoners. Both regular soldiers and guerrillas were killed. Prisoners taken by the United States and other UN forces were sent mainly to two small islands off the peninsula. By November 1950, the UN held more than 130,000 POWs. All of them were screened to determine their political feelings.

The screening of prisoners angered the Chinese. It became a major issue during peace talks. On the UN side, officials did not believe the Chinese were telling the truth about the number of POWs under their control. To this day, the Chinese have never revealed the complete information.

Brainwashing

One great American fear during the Korean War was that the Chinese were brainwashing POWs. In this process, intense psychological questioning and abuse can lead to a person being programmed to give up old beliefs and accept new ones. The few Americans who made propaganda statements for the Chinese seemed to be an example of this. In reality, the Chinese did not brainwash Americans— the process took too much time and could not work on large groups of prisoners.

Diplomacy in Korea, Politics at Home

By summer of 1951, most of the fighting in Korea took place in the hills near the **38th parallel.** Neither side gained a clear advantage, but the battles were still deadly. Each month, the UN forces suffered about 2,500 casualties.

A few months earlier, in May, Soviet and U.S. officials secretly talked about the possibility of ending the war. Leaders on both sides saw how difficult it would be to achieve large gains since both armies were dug in close to the original border. By July, the North Koreans and Chinese also were willing to discuss an **armistice.** On July 10, talks began at Kaesong, just south of the 38th parallel.

At their camp, U.S. delegates to the Panmunjom peace talks plan their strategy for another armistice meeting.

The talks at Kaesong and Panmunjom

The Soviet Union did not attend the talks, since it was not directly involved in the fighting. The North Koreans and Chinese, however, kept in contact with the Soviets. U.S. military officers, along with one South Korean, represented the UN. Each side distrusted the other.

By the end of July, the two sides had agreed to the issues they would discuss. These included how to arrange a cease-fire, create a demilitarized zone, and return prisoners to their homelands. Working out the details of these points began in November at a second set of talks at Panmunjom. After some conflict, both sides finally seemed to agree on where to draw the border between the two Koreas once the armistice was signed. The POW problem proved the most difficult one to solve.

The Americans insisted that **communist** POWs should have the freedom to choose where to go once released. China wanted all its soldiers back without any conditions. The two sides also argued over the number of prisoners held. The Chinese POW lists had far fewer prisoners than the UN officials claimed were held. Unable to solve the issue, the peace talks dragged. At times, the two sides sat silently across from each other for hours. Meanwhile, the fighting continued, and by fall 1952, the talks had stopped.

The presidential election of 1952

Back in the United States, Americans were losing interest in the war. Voters were also losing patience with President Truman. The firing of MacArthur, the charges made by Joseph McCarthy and his supporters, and the **stalemate** in the war made Truman's popularity plummet. In 1952, the president said he would not seek reelection.

In the summer, the Democrats chose Adlai Stevenson as their candidate for president. The Republicans picked General Dwight Eisenhower. Like Truman, Eisenhower insisted the United States keep the option of using nuclear weapons. Peace talks did not resume until April 1953.

In the November 1952 presidential election, Dwight Eisenhower won in a landslide, losing only nine states to his opponent, Adlai Stevenson.

Dwight D. Eisenhower

President Dwight D. Eisenhower (1890–1969) was a graduate of the U.S. Military Academy at West Point, and he once worked as an aide to Douglas MacArthur. During World War II, Eisenhower led the U.S. Army in Europe and commanded the famous D-Day invasion of France in 1944. After the war, he briefly served as the president of Columbia University in New York. Eisenhower returned to active duty in 1951 as supreme commander of the North Atlantic Treaty Organization. The United States had created this military alliance to prevent the spread of communism in Western Europe.

As president, Eisenhower eventually ended the war in Korea. He also continued the military build-up that was meant to stop the Soviet Union from expanding its power. And Eisenhower deepened the U.S. involvement in Vietnam, another Asian country where communists battled against pro-American forces.

The Korean People and the War

As deadly as the Korean War was for soldiers on the battlefield, it was even worse for civilians living on the **peninsula.** In both North Korea and South Korea, people fled their homes to avoid the war, sometimes crossing from one country to the other. A total of several million civilians were killed, and disease and starvation added to the death toll. Although death was common on both sides of the **38th parallel,** the war's impact on civilians varied somewhat in the two Koreas.

Civilians in the South

South Koreans who could not escape battles that were fought near their homes faced danger from exploding shells and stray bullets. But the civilians also feared direct attacks by soldiers from both sides. In the early part of the war, as the NKPA pushed south, North Korean soldiers killed people suspected of supporting Syngman Rhee's government. In some cases, the soldiers killed hundreds of people at a time, although the official North Korean policy was to "reeducate" the civilians and turn them into **communists.**

South Koreans also faced violence from their own army and police forces. The communists had supporters in the south, and **guerrillas** were always a threat. But the Rhee government used the war as an excuse to arrest—and kill—people suspected of opposing Rhee and his policies, as well as genuine supporters of North Korea. Thousands of innocent people were also caught up in this effort. The ROK set up camps to hold those suspected of supporting the North Koreans. A reporter from London wrote that in one camp he saw "hundreds of [people]; they were skeletal ... **manacled** to each other with chains, cringing . . . in piles of garbage."

Life in the North

As the war moved across the 38th parallel, North Koreans faced some of the same violence that

Some South Korean women and children were held at the prison camps set up by the Rhee government for political prisoners and suspected guerrillas.

had gone on in the south. North Korean troops killed their own civilians suspected of aiding the UN forces. Most of the civilian deaths, however, came from the air, as the United States's bombs and napalm fell on both military and civilian areas. The U.S. Air Force also dropped bombs designed not to explode right away. People emerged from shelters after a raid, thinking they were safe, then were killed by these delayed explosions.

A U.S. B-26 bomber scores a direct hit on a church where the North koreans stored explosives.

In November 1950, General MacArthur ordered U.S. planes to bomb every village, town, city, and factory within a large part of North Korea. His idea was to destroy the country's industries and the people's will to fight. The bombing increased as the war went on, and towns were almost completely destroyed. Pyongyang had a population of about 500,000 when the war started. A year later, it was down to 50,000.

To escape the bombing, North Koreans sometimes lived in caves and holes in the ground. They built virtual underground cities, with factories, stores, and hospitals. The activity that went on above ground, including farming, usually took place at night.

A series of heavy U.S. bombing raids in June 1952 destroyed North Korea's main power plants and dams. Large areas of the country went without power for the rest of the war. Attacks on civilians in Pyongyang also increased at this time, with 6,000 people reportedly killed in one attack. Despite the heavy bombing, the North Korean government refused to give in and agree to an armistice.

A view from the North

The bombers came without warning . . . You found dead people everywhere. There was hardly a single house left standing. They bombed the big cities, villages, and the countryside in the same way. I saw it all with my own eyes.

Yan Von Sik, North Korean soldier

Later Battles

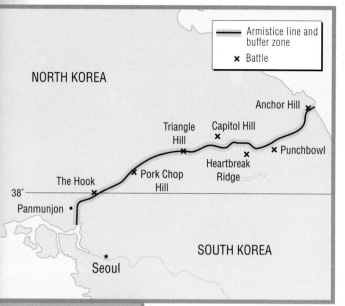

Map legend:
— Armistice line and buffer zone
× Battle

NORTH KOREA

Anchor Hill ×
Triangle Hill ×
Capitol Hill ×
× Punchbowl
Heartbreak Ridge ×
The Hook ×
× Pork Chop Hill
38°
Panmunjon •
SOUTH KOREA
★ Seoul

This map shows the sites of several of the bloodiest battles fought during the last two years of the Korean War.

The stalemate along the **38th parallel** marked the longest phase of the Korean War. It lasted from the summer of 1951 until 1953. This part of the Korean War has sometimes been compared to World War I, since both armies were dug into trenches that were hard to attack. The fighting was difficult, and neither side could gain a clear advantage for long. Most of the fighting took place on and around various hills. Military commanders knew them by numbers, but journalists and soldiers often gave them nicknames.

Heartbreak Ridge

As of August 1951, the NKPA controlled a series of hills near an area called the Punchbowl. The UN drove the North Koreans off Hill 983 in fierce fighting that gave the hill a new name—Bloody Ridge. The communist forces then pulled back to Hill 931. For weeks, the UN troops assaulted it and other surrounding hills, which as a group became known as Heartbreak Ridge. U.S. troops aided by French forces finally took control of the ridge in mid-October, ending one of the deadliest campaigns of the war. UN troops suffered an estimated 3,700 casualties, while the North Koreans and a Chinese division lost at least five times more.

Triangle Hill

The fighting at Heartbreak Ridge marked the last major UN offensive in Korea. For the next year, the fighting was light along the 38th parallel, as the two sides discussed the cease fire at Panmunjom. But then, in May 1952, General Mark Clark replaced Ridgway as the UN commander. When the peace talks broke down in October 1952, Clark launched Operation Showdown, the first big ground offensive since Heartbreak Ridge.

The operation's goal was to take three small hills known together as Triangle Hill. In the hills, the Chinese had built a large system of well-defended tunnels and trenches. The fighting dragged on for more than a month. After suffering about 9,000 casualties, the UN had gained very little ground and could not take Triangle Hill.

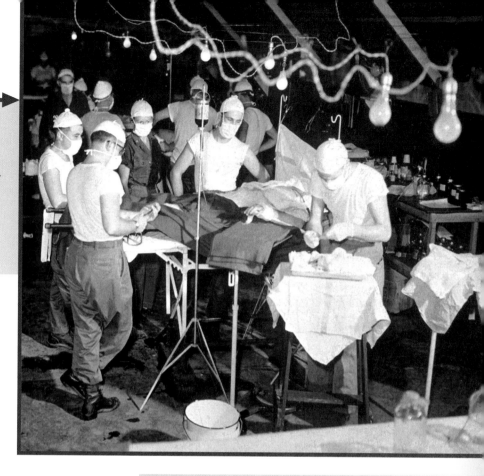

Near the front lines, members of the 8209th Mobile Army Surgical Hospital (MASH) treat a wounded soldier.

Pork Chop Hill

The last major battles of the Korean War took place at Pork Chop Hill, between March and July of 1953. The UN defended the hill against Chinese forces but could not drive them out. Chinese artillery shells exploded as American engineers rebuilt trenches. During one intense battle, a U.S. soldier described how his unit ran out of ammunition, "so we fought them with rifle butts, bayonets, and even fists and helmets." Peace talks had resumed by now, and an armistice seemed likely. Rather than lose more men holding Pork Chop Hill, the UN withdrew on July 10.

Women in War

As in World War II, American women played an important role during the Korean War. The first to arrive were nurses; in July 1950, they helped set up a hospital in Pusan. Others served close to the front at Mobile Army Surgical Hospitals—MASH units— patching wounds and treating the sick. Women served in each branch of the U.S. armed forces, stationed at bases in the Far East, but not in Korea itself. Women worked in such areas as food service, communications, and ran motor pools. A few worked as translators. By 1952, the total number of women on active duty had grown from 29,000 at the start of the war to 46,000.

Peace at Last

By the spring of 1953, Dwight Eisenhower had taken over as the U.S. president and issued his threat to use nuclear weapons, if necessary. More important, however, was the death of Joseph Stalin on March 5. The Soviet leader had wanted to keep the war going as long as possible, to weaken the U.S. military. After his death, other Soviet leaders seemed more willing to discuss peace, and Mao agreed. Important U.S. allies, such as Great Britain and France, also wanted to end the war as quickly as possible.

General Mark Clark, representing the United Nations, signs the armistice on July 27, 1953.

Little Switch

In April 1953, both sides agreed to exchange sick and wounded prisoners. This operation, called Little Switch by the UN, led to the release of more than 6,000 soldiers, mostly Chinese, from UN POW camps, while the Chinese and NKPA turned over about 700 UN soldiers. It also led to the last round of peace talks at Panmunjom.

The Chinese and North Koreans truly wanted peace, but they also kept fighting, hoping to improve their position in the field. When an **armistice** came, the boundary between the two Koreas would fall near wherever each side's troops were located. The **communists** wanted as much land as possible for North Korea.

Rhee fights the peace process

The biggest obstacle to peace, however, was not the communists, but the South Korean leader Syngman Rhee. He refused to accept an armistice that kept Korea divided and hinted that South Korea would keep fighting if the UN troops left. Rhee wanted to unify the country and keep it under his control.

Rhee caused trouble in early June, when he freed thousands of anticommunist North Korean POWs who did not want to return home when the war ended. Rhee's move angered both the United States and the communists, and delayed an armistice agreement. By July, however, the Americans had persuaded Rhee to accept whatever armistice the UN signed with North Korea and China.

UN POWs gain their freedom during Big Switch, the major exchange of prisoners at the end of the Korean War.

The end of the war

The final armistice was signed on July 27, 1953, taking effect that night at 10:01 P.M. South Korea never signed the document, though it agreed to accept the results. Just a few days before, the two sides had agreed on the line that would separate the two Koreas, and on the creation of the demilitarized zone. Starting a few weeks later, the two sides began their final exchange of POWs—the Big Switch, as it was called in the West. More than 100,000 people moved from one side to the other during Big Switch.

In legal terms, the July 1953 armistice was not a peace treaty. Neither side had officially declared war when the Korean conflict began, and neither side agreed to a permanent peace. The Korean War ended with a truce, or temporary end of the fighting. The two Koreas never signed a peace treaty, though they later signed other agreements designed to reduce tensions.

A first taste of peace

At earliest light the troops came up out of the ground to look . . . It was unheard of—standing in the open in daylight. An incredible feeling. I think infantrymen all across the peninsula, on both sides, must have been awed by it. Just the simple, natural act of standing erect in the sunshine . . .and eventually to walk through the land ahead of the trenches, a thing that would have meant sure death twenty-four hours before. That's when we began to realize that it was really over.

Robert Hall, U.S. Marine

The Results of the War

After the armistice was signed, Syngman Rhee said South Korea had the right to begin fighting again after a 90-day period. To help keep the peace, the United States agreed to keep troops in South Korea. About 37,000 U.S. forces were still there as of 2002.

As the fighting finally ended, the two sides began to count their losses. The United States lost more than 53,000 troops. Slightly more than 8,000 troops were listed as missing in action and presumed dead. North Korea and South Korea had, by one estimate, more than three million people killed, including both soldiers and civilians, with another five million left homeless. The Chinese lost probably at least 500,000 troops, and perhaps more than one million.

Winners and losers

The huge death toll came in a war that some historians—and participants—say had no real winner. The North Korean goal was to unify the two Koreas. That mission failed, so in one sense, the UN won. But General MacArthur and other U.S. leaders wanted to end the **communist** rule in the north. Failing to achieve that, the Americans lost.

The Chinese also failed in their main goal, to push the Americans and the anticommunists out of South Korea. Yet they and North Koreans often said the **armistice** was really a surrender by the United Nations. But years after the war, Nikolai Fedorenko, a Soviet diplomat, saw the war as a loss for the communists: "We were unable to impose the socialist system on South Korea, so it was a defeat." The Soviet Union lost in other ways. Its failure to take a more direct effort in the war made China and North Korea closer allies and played a part in souring the relationship between China and the Soviet Union. The war also led to increased spending for defense among the United States and its allies in the **Cold War.** The Soviet Union had to spend large amounts of money to keep pace.

Effects on the United States

Some U.S. military leaders felt their political leaders did not give them the means to truly win the war. Certainly MacArthur felt limited by President Truman. After the war, several military leaders spoke out against the idea of fighting a "limited" war, but the same issue came up again when the United States became involved with the war in Vietnam.

The Korean War increased American suspicions of communist China. Under Eisenhower, the government made it official policy to end the communist government of China. The experience in Korea also influenced the role the United States played in Vietnam. As early as 1950, President Truman sent money and advisers to Vietnam, hoping to build up United States influence and prevent a communist takeover. Once Vietnam won its independence from France in 1954, the United States played an even larger role, still fearful of Soviet and Chinese efforts to spread communism in Asia.

Even as U.S. troops fought in Korea, the first American advisers arrived in Vietnam as early as 1954. Here, a U.S. Army Ranger trains a group of Vietnamese soldiers.

Other UN Losses

Here is a list of the other UN countries that sent military forces to Korea, along with the number of soldiers killed or missing in action. In addition to these countries, several other UN members sent medical personnel.

Country	Killed/Missing in Action	Country	Killed/Missing in Action
Australia	330	Greece	171
Belgium/Luxembourg (joint force)	102	Netherlands	115
Canada	312	New Zealand	34
Colombia	205	Philippines	149
Ethiopia	120	South Africa	36
France	306	Thailand	119
Great Britain	1,973	Turkey	824

The Two Koreas After the War

After the Korean War, South Korea remained closely tied to the United States and pursued capitalism. North Korea, meanwhile, slowly tried to distance itself from China and the Soviet Union, even though all three countries practiced **communism.** Both Koreas kept strong military forces, just in case war began again.

The struggle for wealth and democracy

The war destroyed the wealth of South Korea's upper classes, along with homes, factories, and buildings. The United States helped rebuild the country, pouring in billions of dollars of aid. Koreans also worked hard and saved their money. Slowly the South Korean economy began to improve. Companies well known in the United States today, such as Hyundai and Samsung, either started after the war or grew tremendously during the postwar boom. By the 1980s, South Korea was one of the richest nations in Asia.

Since the Korean War, students, shopkeepers, and other South Koreans have sometimes staged violent protests against their government.

In politics, however, South Korea struggled to follow the American model and build a democratic society. After the war, Rhee continued to rule harshly. In 1960, protests against his rule forced him to resign. The next year, the Korean military took over the government. One of the generals in the **junta,** Park Chung Hee, was elected president in 1963, but the country still lacked true democracy. Starting in the 1970s, South Koreans frequently protested against their government, demanding more political freedom. Greater democracy finally came during the 1990s.

North Korea alone

In the North, Kim Il Sung continued to rule as a dictator until his death in 1994. Kim devoted the country's resources to heavy industry, such as steel, and the manufacture of weapons. Kim's form of communism helped the North Koreans build a clean, well-ordered country. But under Kim, North Koreans had no political freedom and little economic freedom.

Kim wanted North Korea to be completely self-reliant. Although at first it got some aid from China and the Soviet Union, the country increasingly cut itself off from the rest of the world. "Hold fast to independence," Kim once said. That independence, along with great secrecy, led to suspicions in the West about North Korea's plans. The fear of North Korea grew during the 1980s and 1990s. North Korea began producing plutonium, the material used to make some nuclear weapons. The country also tested missiles that could carry these weapons. Since 1994, North Korea has resisted efforts to let international groups inspect its nuclear program.

Under Kim's son, Kim Jong II, North Korea was forced to have more contact with other countries. A famine from 1995 to 1998 killed as many as two million North Koreans. Kim turned to the United States, among other nations, for food donations. Still, North Koreans remain mostly isolated from the rest of the world.

Using simple hand tools, North Korean students plant trees. Although modern in some ways, the North Korean economy is not as advanced as South Korea's.

Easing tensions on the peninsula

Distrust remains between the two Koreas, but over the years, they have tried to improve their relations. In July 1972, the two Koreas agreed to try to create one country again, using peaceful means, but they never achieved this goal. In 1991, the two countries said they would work together on some economic issues. Korean leaders also agreed to let families living in the two countries visit each other for the first time since the end of the war.

The greatest step for peace on the peninsula came in 2000. Kim Jong II met with South Korean president Kim Dae Jung—the first meeting ever between leaders of the two Koreas. The two men pledged to work for peace and reunite their countries. Even so, both sides remain prepared for war, and tensions flared again in 2002, when North Korean and South Korean ships clashed in the Yellow Sea.

Kim Dae Jung

Born in 1932, Kim Dae Jung was one of the leaders of political reform in South Korea. His work to promote democracy led to several attempts on his life. He also served time in prison because of his beliefs. In 1997, Kim was elected president of South Korea. For his efforts to promote peaceful relations with North Korea, Kim won the Nobel Peace Prize in 2000.

The United States and the Two Koreas Today

Thanks to their military and economic ties, the United States and South Korea remain close allies. U.S. relations with North Korea, however, have sometimes been stormy.

North Korea and the end of the Cold War

In 1991, **communism** ended in the Soviet Union, which split into separate countries. The end of the Soviet Union marked the end of the **Cold War.** For the first time, Western scholars were allowed to read secret Soviet documents about the Korean War and other events. These documents shed new light on the start of the war and Soviet actions to help the Chinese and North Koreans.

The Soviet documents showed that Kim Il Sung was the main force behind the June 1950 invasion. Although Joseph Stalin talked about waging worldwide war against capitalism, he was cautious about a war in Korea.

A North Korean threat?

During the late 1980s and early 1990s, U.S. presidents worried about North Korea's program to develop nuclear weapons. By 1994, the situation had reached a crisis. Some U.S. scholars and government officials feared another war might start on the peninsula. Talks between the two sides helped end the crisis and improve relations between the two countries for a time. Still, U.S. military experts predicted the North Koreans would eventually build nuclear weapons that could reach the United States.

When George W. Bush became president in 2001, he considered North Korea a threat to U.S. security. Bush's suspicions of North Korea increased after the September 11, 2001, terrorist attacks on New York and Washington, D.C. Bush was convinced that North Korea was one of three nations that sponsored terrorist acts around the world. North Korea was also considered a threat because of its efforts to build weapons of mass destruction. In 2002, North Korea announced it had broken an agreement stop its development of nuclear weapons.

Remembering the Korean War

The ongoing tensions with North Korea remind Americans that in some ways the Cold War is not over. The current situation also suggests that the United States still has an important role to play on the Korean **peninsula.** But the Korean War is a distant memory to many people. In the United States, the war has been called both the "unknown war" and the "forgotten war."

In the United States, Korean War veterans have tried to educate Americans about the thousands of military troops who lost their lives fighting in Korea. Some veterans host websites providing information about the war. The U.S. government also honored the dead with in 1995, with the opening of the Korean War Veterans Memorial in Washington D.C. These efforts help Americans understand how North Korea and South Korea became so important in U.S. foreign relations. The ongoing education also reminds people of the millions who died in Korea.

The Korean War Veterans Memorial features statues of nineteen soldiers, as well a wall of carved faces representing many of the troops who served.

The No Gun Ri controversy

In 1999, the Associated Press (AP) claimed to have found several eyewitnesses who had seen U.S. troops kill civilians during the Korean War near the village of No Gun Ri. Soon more newspapers wrote about this supposed "massacre." The AP won the Pulitzer Prize, the highest honor in journalism, for the story. Some historians, however, asserted that the AP had gotten the story wrong. The controversy led the United States and South Korea to investigate what happened at No Gun Ri. The U.S. officials concluded that there was no evidence of U.S. soldiers killing Korean civilians.

Korean War Timeline

1882	The United States and Korea sign their first trade treaty.
1910	Japan takes control of Korea.
1919	Koreans violently protest Japanese rule.
1945	Soviet troops drive the Japanese out of Korea. The **38th parallel** becomes the border of Soviet- and U.S.-controlled areas. Syngman Rhee returns to Korea from the United States. Kim Il Sung also returns after fighting for the Soviet Union during World War II. The **Cold War** begins.
1948	The United Nations conducts elections in South Korea. The Republic of Korea forms in the south, while Kim Il Sung leads the new Democratic People's Republic of Korea in the north. Rebellions and **guerrilla** fighting break out in the south.
1949	The Soviet Union tests its first nuclear weapon. A civil war in China ends with **communists** controlling most of the country.
1950	In the United States, the Rosenbergs are arrested as Soviet spies. Senator Joseph McCarthy says some government officials are communists. With Soviet help, the North Koreans launch a surprise attack on South Korea. The UN votes to send troops to help South Korea. U.S. general Douglas MacArthur is named UN commander and wages a **counterattack** from Inchon. UN troops push the North Koreans back across the 38th parallel and come close to China. The communist Chinese join North Korea's side. The combined communist forces push the UN troops southward, past the 38th parallel.
1951	UN troops finally stop the Chinese counterattack. President Harry Truman removes MacArthur as UN commander. The first peace talks begin. U.S. battle units are **integrated** for the first time. UN troops launch last major counterattack of the war in fighting near Heartbreak Ridge.
1952	North Korea accuses UN of using germ warfare. Uprisings break out at South Korean prisoner-of-war camps. Truman does not run for reelection. U.S. begins massive bombing campaign in North Korea. Dwight Eisenhower is elected the next U.S. president and makes a short visit to Korea.
1953	Both sides exchange wounded and sick POWs during Little Switch. Peace talks resume. Last major battle occurs, at Pork Chop Hill. The two sides sign an **armistice** and create the **Demilitarized Zone.** Big Switch marks the major exchange of POWs.
1960	South Koreans protest Syngman Rhee's rule, forcing him from office.
1991	North Korea and South Korea pledge to work together on certain issues.
1994	North Korea refuses to cooperate with inspections of is nuclear program. Former U.S. president Jimmy Carter visits the country. Kim Il Sung dies and is replaced by his son, Kim Jong Il.
1997	Kim Dae Jung, a reformer, wins the presidential election in South Korea.
2000	Kim Dae Jung and Kim Jong Il meet to discuss unifying the two Koreas in the future.
2002	President George W. Bush accuses North Korea of supporting terrorism and being a threat to U.S. security. North Korea announces its plans to resume development of nuclear weapons.

Further Reading

Nonfiction

Ashabranner, Brent K. *Remembering Korea: The Korean War Veterans Memorial.* Brookfield, Conn.: Twenty-First Century Books, 2001.

Benson, Sonia. *Korean War: Almanac and Primary Sources.* Detroit: UXL, 2002.

Burgan, Michael. *Cold War: The Hot Conflicts.* Austin: Raintree Steck-Vaughn Publishers, 2001.

Dolan, Edward. *America in the Korean War.* Brookfield, Conn.: Millbrook Press, 1998.

Zeinert, Karen. *McCarthy and the Fear of Communism in American History.* Springfield, N.J.: Enslow Publishers, 1998.

Fiction

Choi, Sook Nyul. *Year of Impossible Goodbyes.* Boston, Mass.: Houghton Mifflin, 1991.

Park, Linda Sue. *When My Name Was Keoko.* New York: Clarion Books, 2002.

Websites

United States Korean War 50th Anniversary Commemoration
http://korea50.army.mil

Korean War Veterans National Museum and Library
http://www.theforgottenvictory.org/

United States Department of Defense, Korea: The Land of Morning Calm
http://www.defenselink.mil/specials/korea/

Glossary

38th parallel line of latitude marking the border between North Korea and South Korea

ally a friend or supporter

ammunition bullets and other objects fired from guns and artillery

amphibious capable of being used both on land and in water; in war, an assault launched by sea on a land target

annex take control of through force or the threat of force

armistice halt to the fighting during war

artillery large, mobile guns that can fire long distances

atomic bomb nuclear weapon that uses the energy created when atoms of uranium or plutonium are split apart

boycott refuse to do something

capitalism economic system that favors private ownership of business and freedom from government controls

casualties soldiers killed, wounded, or missing in action, or taken prisoner

Cold War period of hostility or tension between the United States and the Soviet Union after World War II

communism economic system that favors public or government ownership of business. A person who supports communism is a communist.

Communist Party the governing group of the Soviet Union

containment U.S. policy after World War II that focused on stopping the spread of communism around the world

counterattack fighting begun to move forward against an enemy that had been advancing

Demilitarized Zone (DMZ) area on either side of the border between North Korea and South Korea where troops and weapons are not allowed

diplomacy words and actions between governments designed to ease tensions and create good relations

draft the selection of young men at random to join an army

dynasty a family that passes rule of country from one generation to the next

empire large areas of land controlled by a single powerful nation

exile state of being forced to leave one's native country

guerrilla   fighter who uses "hit and run" tactics, blending in with civilians and using surprise to attack larger enemy forces

hydrogen bomb   highly destructive nuclear weapon that uses the energy created when hydrogen atoms join together

ideological   relating to basic political and social beliefs that help shape attitudes or actions

integrate   make open to all races

junta   a government led by small group of military officers who seize power

manacled   restrained

McCarthyism   During the Cold War, a movement to remove communist influences from American society; named after Senator Joseph McCarthy

nationalized   taken over by the government

Nazi   a member of National Socialist Party of Germany, led by Adolf Hitler

nuclear   relating to energy produced by splitting or combining atoms; comes from nucleus, the core of an atom

peninsula   a large area of land that is surrounded by water on three sides

perimeter   the outer edge of an area

propaganda   information spread by a government or group to influence others' thoughts or actions; often the information is false or only partially true

refugees   people forced to leave their homes or country, usually because of war or natural disaster

retreat   turn away from the front lines of a battle

segregate   separate by race

Security Council   the most powerful branch of the United Nations

superpowers   large countries with strong militaries and much influence over other countries

stalemate   a war that cannot be won by either participant

tracer   ammunition that marks its flight by smoke or fire

veto   forbid or prevent from happening

Index